Everything I Touch Is—& Isn't —You

a poetry collaboration

David Allen Sullivan & Ignatius Valentine Aloysius

Everything I Touch Is—& Isn't —You

a poetry collaboration

David Allen Sullivan & Ignatius Valentine Aloysius

ROADSIDE PRESS

Cover design & layout: True Ideas, Evanston, IL

The text is set in Athelas & Azo Sans

Library of Congress Control Number: 2026934566
ISBN: 979-8-9996256-9-4

ROADSIDE PRESS
Meredosia, Illinois

DEDICATIONS

David:
To friends and family who've kept me afloat

Ignatius:
For my parents. For Cynthia.
For ancestors known & unknown

AUTHORS' NOTE:

This second collection of poems continues from our first collaboration in *Salt Pruning*, where the poems are woven as responses to each other's poems and include further explorations of our new inventive form—the Golden Sliver—arising from Terrance Hayes' original Golden Shovel poetic form. The poems sometimes share a theme, or reference the same incident, & some borrow lines or words from poems preceding them. A Golden Sliver threads together a single sentence from words inside a previous poem, which become the end words of each line in the new poem, as well as the final line. The newest form, Golden Shoots & Ladders, borrows a line or words from a previous poem, & can be read vertically, as well as horizontally.

The back-&-forth nature of the project can be followed in the Table of Contents, where the titles of David's poems are flush left, & Ignatius' are indented. "Waiting," the final poem is co-written by both poets, each contributing a responsive verse.

ACKNOWLEDGMENTS:

Allium: A Journal of Poetry & Prose: Pourquoi me réveil; My Irish Great Great Grandfather, Turned Away from Ellis Island, Entered the United States Via Canada; Heart, A Patched Up Place
Blue Lake Review: Every Surface Visible
Hungry Hill: Poets meet Politics poetry competition (Second Place): Wouldn't Give
#Ranger: Experimental Poetry: talking sticks   taking stock; On Scene Eyes   Unseen I's
Red Wheelbarrow: The last poem's "Horse" section
Roadside Assistance: A Roadside Press Reader Anthology: Inhabit the Gone Song, Self-evacuation, Strike Home, Horoscopes of Sentient Creatures

Deep gratitude to the poets, loved ones, and friends who helped us along the way. Thank you to Roadside Press for giving our second collaboration a home, and to the zines where some poems were first published; as well, to Cynthia Kerby for the stellar art which graces our cover. We appreciate you, Mary Biddinger, Taylor Byas, Roxi Power, and Brad Crenshaw.

TABLE OF CONTENTS

III. Born from Shells & Tinder

I.

Still Your Breath

Inhabit the Gone Song

—hiking Mount Tamalpais

This is the place you've always wanted
      to be, though you had no idea
you had to come through hell &
      highwater to get here: playground
beatings, cheating on tests, marriages,
      divorces, a still birth, the roll call
of addictions. You're here on this ridge
      trail, mist obscuring the view
you came for & then seeing the mist
      itself as beautiful. Angel hair lichen
wears a hem of raindrops & spider lines
      are outlined in drips. Pines spike
& mellow in the mist. Breathe in
      the cool air. Exhale your heat. Exfoliate
like the stone you're scrabbling up.
      Every moment is born from within
if you can just attend. Still your breath.
      Listen to the rolling sine-wave passage
of the bird, & its two-note toggling
      for companionship. Be in the singing
whether or not you get an answer.

Self-evacuation

Sometimes, it gets too hard to live & simply be
in one place, simply do one thing in life & stay in
the body's house, all-inside with songs from the
past plastered all over my walls, its ghosts singing
of my self-evacuation from the homeland, whether
the doors & windows are shut or not. Just do this or
that; take more jobs, go on & earn a buck to live, not
suffer the immigrant's long heartache, which you
see but can't talk about now. I thought you'd get
someone else, someone better. You deserve that in an
instant but stay. Days hug a future w/ art's answer.

A Golden Shovel of David Allen Sullivan's Inhabit the Gone Song

Strike Home

Be in uncertainties, mysteries, doubts, without any irritable reaching
after fact and reason.
                                                    John Keats' letter, 1817

I'm a paltry host without my caravan of ghosts
those who chose to clamber in-board, singing
of what they lost/tossed, bones become flutes of
joy/grief, hamstrings wring the string section, my
skull's a bulbous talking drum. Did self-evacuation
permit their tunes to invade my hollows? Songs from
pasts I don't own but walk among, humming the
shivery hit from 1959—*when the shark bites...* Home
in on the blade, be brave enough to see it land—
& does it matter what's permitted? Do I ask whether
sense seamed shut my ribs? I try closing the doors
of perception, but a hand slips in, & windows
are rattled in their casements. Horror movies are
already in me, I reel with memories I can't shut
out, must house what I'm given. I must take it in or
be taken on—there's no slipping this Gordian knot.

Golden Shovel of Ignatius Valentine Aloysius' Self-evacuation

Horoscopes of Sentient Creatures

What past are we preserving for the future
we would claim?
> ~from "Exhibits in the Archive of Sinking and Melting"
> by Jared Beloff in *Who Will Cradle Your Head*

We'll step carefully in the backyard, won't we? Oh, the horror
of crushing these tiny ants, pushing up sand mounds, like movies
of hot stillness in the Sahara show. We'll fan away the flies; they're
always here, rising from rich surroundings like ascetics already
part & parcel of our being, entering buzz-clad in the air felt in me,
while the basic laws of existence press in from all directions. I reel
from hero-worship, I reel, but we must adore something. We'll sink
with chronologies of truth, if their public factories keep exhibiting
memories found melting on sidewalks & inside shut ribs, casements,
in blinds, where spiders (I can't watch!) come unknowingly to die.
Read books, shut out false statements raising pointless questions of
our reflexes. We must mourn the senseless killing! Imperfect is the
blade life sprung from, & a house without rules labors against the
horoscope's wheel. Sentience is what we have & can lose in a crush-
ing minute, while cells slip in & out. I'm a soft creature so &
no explosion of kindness can say justice is a given.

Practicing Ahimsa in the Napolry

I tiptoe past catastrophes, genuflect over car wrecks, I'm
trying to hurt things less & less, but still I'm an a-
ccessory to another heart hurt. My whipping words soft-
ly implode in my love's ear. What unseen creature-
s have my running shoes smeared? How do the Jainists do it? So
at peace they offer up their blood to mosquitoes &
bless their progeny. I want to be more & less. I'm no-
where near transcendence. I can still see the explosion
of purple when the crushed cochineal bug received a shot of
lime juice. What's collected & killed for beauty? Is kindness
doing the least harm? or the greatest good? No god says
there's a remedy for living that exempts me. Injustice
can't be named unless it names me too. The wheel is
turning when the zapotec net's thrown over the cacti. I'm a-
wash in undiscovered colors. Can a pinched death be forgiven?

Golden Shovel of Ignatius Valentine Aloysius' Horoscopes of Sentient Creatures

Facing Redemption

The butterflies have come. So cute! Summer's masterstroke is no small wonder as these winged chariots descend from the lips of god looking for sweetness & praise. Surely, this small garden is lacking, says the cultivator. My backyard has poor housing for butterflies, & there's so much water from the week's rain, but still they come. The milkweed's a trail of quiet despair, downy software sheltering in near shade. A remedy once used to be a cluster of red Monarda sparkling like fireworks for the bees, too, every year in delirious sunlight, until conditions for living changed & red's roots fought a culture war, almost lost. Friends that know me say I too have changed, gone quieter & distant. As if life exempts the redeeming ones from rising fast & sweet as my joe-pye-weeds tall as me.

Golden Shovel of David Allen Sullivan's Practicing Ahimsa in the Napolry

Inner Gardens of Unearthly Delights

Hinges	swivel	a round	a thin rod	open closed	butterflies
whine	hips	of roses	pierce(s)	hands	lips
wetted	dance	rings	leaves	leave a	sweetness
edges	the glass	her	mouth	kissed(kiss)	housing
words	she will	k(not)	speak(s)	of	rain
will	fall	above	her head	whirring	soft where
we fall	a part	what	com(es)	down	sparkling
inward	en-(ing)	counter	ing	wine(s)	delirious
pause	glance(s)	exchanged	&	throat	roots
around	for her	center(ed)	everything's	gone	quiet
us?	what?	wetness	blushes	a bloom	rising fast
butterfly lips	*sweetness*	*housing rain*	*soft where*	*delirious*	*roots rise*

Golden Shoots & Ladders of Ignatius Valentine Aloysius's Facing Redemption

Hinges

Success feels gossamer thin, fixed in harmony w/ fate like hinges
to a heavy door, organized in life's remarkable capsules, loose hips
moving until some pill-glass breaks, because medicine runs rings
around all superstitions like economic necessity...in the mouth
in the stomach in all our prejudices passing through conduits of
adulation flooding the world with impossible reasons. I am soft-
made, no matter what they tell you men should be/are, set down
by their/my own defeating journeys of lessons taught, encountering
guilt & chance, the acknowledging of mistakes past, & those glances
from bloodline hand to appealing hand. Trust is mine, it works around
hinges hips rings mouth of soft down encountering glances around us.

Golden Sliver of David Allen Sullivan's Inner Gardens of Unearthly Delights

Unhinged

—in Florence with Mina

In 1447 Paolo Uccello painted the flood
on plaster: it roils in, gray coils of the
gray-cloaked sky whip at the world
furiously. The ark's a massive hull with
rivets & thick bracing whose impossible
walls are beat on by outcasts. Their reasons
for entry can't compete with the storm. I
have always chosen the rains. What am
I, but another outsider, trying to soft-
en my own heart first. Uccello made
agony his subject, their histrionic *no-*
's! trapped in the strict geometry of matter
so linear it squelches spirit. What
will become of us? Why won't they
open their doors? We're all here, tell-
ing our tales, each of us pained. You
are no better than the calliope of men
nursing their addictions. We should
undo the doors & join them, let us be
what each of these rain-flailing men are.

Golden Shovel of Ignatius Valentine Aloysius's Hinges

Ally of the Sublunar

The stretched first sound of a sparrow leaves its throat as you
lay still deep, darkness wandering around you in bed. These are
night's measures still pressing in a fundamental way, making no
other remarks to turn the light on in your head. Sparrow's better
off starting early in the quiet custody of its nest, no more than
a dozen feet away from your pillows. Life's propaganda thrums in the
clamshell of your dreams, begs a fight for social justice or calliope('s)
gift seeing you in print, shouts too much war, fakery, religion; & of
truth, says so little's bursting through the cracks. It's much worse, men
are doing unthinkable acts against women back home, & no nursing
can ever change patriarchy's rule, its fundamental views. You left their
superstitions behind, took on other pains & morality's wild addictions.

Golden Shovel of David Allen Sullivan's Unhinged

water worships   courses   over stone   spangles   a dozen

plump koi   turning   over light   beneath your   feet

& one   so old & red   in flayed tatters eyes turn   away

still you see   like blood   over turned   bodies   breath from

him   gone   underground   stilled   you're(your)

these   blunt   forced up-   swellings ripped pillows

pained   flesh   swelled   your father's   life's

dementia   repeating   rote   phrases &   propaganda

imbibed   from the tribe's self-   assessed talk that thrums

stories   poorly   contained   encased   in

made up   fabricated   fronts   lies   the

speaker   invents(ions) armor scales   forced open   clamshell

speaks   as if   butt of a   joke that tells   of

what no   one   can(ned)   riffle   you're(your)

(the)one speaks   off the hook   of language   fishing   watery dreams

Golden Shoots & Ladders of Ignatius Valentine Aloysius' Ally of the Sublunar

Fruit Enmeshed

Take the papaya for instance, bite-sized pink pained
pulp pieces of old memories drunken victory flesh
flopping worlds not meant forever in rounds un-swelled
like weak opinions, as sermons, jobs done burning your father's
sincerity effigy to live another yearly episode in life's
complicating stamina determined to advance every bite dementia
hunger & health state(ments) like fossils' cries repeating
the ravaging soul-death petitioning sand-locked for peace words rote
wrote by sign pining for policies of reverence & hope phrases

Golden Shovel of David Allen Sullivan's talking sticks   taking stock

Rethreshed/thrashed

*Love is the will to extend one's self for the purpose
of nurturing one's own or another's spiritual growth.*

bell hooks

Pressed into my hand,
flare of a maple leaf,
leather-soft, creased,
a veined, topographic
map—countries I've
traversed & cursed—
what I took from them,
what I couldn't/can't

              take

back. I lean into what
gives way, find my-
self falling. I've been
altered irrevocably—
am each day—can't be
other then this state of
longing, these tiers
of layered memories,

            the

lessons of lessening.
I hear a tiny, tinny,
rafter-hung bell, see
a fish-shaped clapper
the breeze wheels to
set ringing. Beneath,
a monk buries his blade
on the other side of a

            papaya—

it rings, stump-stuck.
Glowing fruit halves
rock. Docked boats

spilling their black
cache of seeds in slick
liquid—oddly sensual.
Why's all this still here?
What's memory
                          for
but to layer up what
will soon start dim-
inishing? The way
my dementied father
started leaving even as
his body bulked up.
Reliving his Dad's
death he told of an
                          instance
when the mother of
his friend gave him
permission to cry—
said it felt like a per-
formance, his mac-
&-cheese clotted
by snotty tears. Hole
in his portion was
                          bite-sized
but never filled, because
he rushed out of there,
stripped a branch to make
a switch & gave hell
to an undeserving bush.
Said it felt good to do
something bad. After-
wards, hands raw &
                          pink
he swore he'd never
let anyone see him

that weak. But Dad,
you showed me, by
coughing up details,
that toughness is a thin
covering, a primer paint—
underneath we're all still
                    pained.

Golden Sliver of Ignatius Valentine Aloysius' Fruit Enmeshed

A Better World

The Joe Pye Weed will do just about anything
to get attention, even rise past the wooden
fence, its words thrown in every direction, just
so it can draw in every butterfly & bee.
                       I've
written this thought in a Twitter post already,
feeling privately lost today with indifference
to the world, feeling shame, my guilt having
                          been
instilled in my DNA before the C-Section done
untied me from compression, & my now-dead
mother's more relieved of yet another burden
imposed on her tired body, changing mood,
color, like the clusters of Joe Pye Weed also
do before my eyes daily. Now mauve, they're
                          altered
as I am also altered by the desire to rise high
past the wooden fences of my peculiar past
determined to hold me in still. It is possible
to become something better, more beautiful
than the ugliness that molded me fully &
                        irrevocably
with its sharpness & taint. This morning, I
awakened from the night's deep sleep &
thought: it's a better world out there, where
I saw the original wonder of sweet love coursing
happily through me, & I took it lying down.

Golden Shovel of David Allen Sullivan's Rethreshed/thrashed

An Aortic Aneurysm Graft

I spy his cockle-shaped, protuberant heart—
saw it lub-dubbing on the monitor, & imagined
the original inside Carlyle's chest, a wild &
wonderful double-fisted hammer, a wo-
of-sweet-woof dog thumping its cage. I'm in
love with the pulse of his new being, blood
coursing interior rivers where oceans of sense drift
happily consanguineous past tide-talk's nets.

Through it all, those mis-named heart cockles tickle
me, how Latin's cochleae cordis shucked linguistic seas,
& I delight in the shell game slippage that
took it in, that makes my friend pun—he's
lying in bed, grinning, wrestling words that come
down to this—inside-out—opening-closing fists.

Reverse Golden Shovel of Ignatius Valentine Aloysius' A Better World

Lessons on Morality

Change has come too slowly, body & mind affirming that I'm
more or less corrected from a self-plundering past. Paths made in-
tentionally had their freedoms taken away, their speeches un-love(d)
& newsstand-muted, muzzled—because morality misused with
the slightest inversion needs a censor. Change found me, forced the
tide, made a new human from this soul of mine. Time's got each pulse,
time has his number. Now he goes to the university, to the bookstore, of-
fers up a smile & good conversation to anyone who will listen to his
opinion. He happens to make them feel good, & feels good too, the new
heart & considerate person that he's become, moving as a spirit-being
—He's all of me & I'm in love with the pulse of his new being, blood.

Golden Sliver of David Allen Sullivan's An Aortic Aneurysm Graft

Eyes	(g)rise-	up	another	body
ear-	ly-	turn	up	of
a nose	bear	in(on-)	mind what	mine
means	possess-	ion	having in	time
what	isn't	sticks like	thick-	ticks
we let	in-	elegant-	ly	each
in-	herent-	ly	separate	pulse
coalesce	able	disassembled	stills	time
freezes	subject	rounds as	object	has
hunger	succor(s)	drive(n)	that	his
long-	ing for more	god	is his	number

Golden Shoots & Ladders of Ignatius Valentine Aloysius' Lessons on Morality

In meditation I sit still

with eyes open, fixed on all that
                    I admire in the small garden out back. We
weren't ashamed to get our hands dirty
                    for it, the care given. Pink anemones let
the bees hover now; a dozen bees
                    go rolling in flowers' pollen, held in
wild ecstasy by desire, touch, soft
                    bathing without censorship. Water's elegantly
dancing 24/7 in the old stone fountain
                    with a delicate jump & sparkle; each
blade of failed-irises rises yet, as morning's
                    yellow light sweeps across, inherently
built for understanding beyond bodies
                    enmeshed in webs of consumption: separate
I am not from all that. Push aside the
                    thought! The air is witness to my warm pulse,
springing in my view in pockets through
                    greenery & in the way its coalesce-able
wonder speaks & moves. Our thoughts
                    are being tested. We're being disassembled
even as I count each breath down & visualize
                    success playing out in future stills
of color. What does it matter in the end?
                    Going deeper, in death my mind my time
will be wiped clean to forage new begin-
                    nings when that moment rips, freezes.

Golden Shovel of David Allen Sullivan's On Scene Eyes   Unseen I's

un/delineated

in the body's blessed confines   we   a-
            ccess damage   seed successes   dozen-
ed like slo-mo   pollen-plastered   bees
            we lumber heavily   towards our   go-
al   now we've had   our fill   of rolling in
            clover pastures   caressing   flowers
that used us   to export   their seed pollen-
            packets   we insure   the world's held
together   by holding our histories   in
            our bodies   letting them speak   of wild-
ings   that ushered in   acres   of ecstasy
            despite failings & fears   we're shielded by
what landed us   here   it's not   our desire-
            s we need to ditch   but all those   touch-
es that can no longer touch us   eluded like soft
            feathers held in a hard hand   we're bathing
in what could be   heart's hedonism   without
            fear of reprisal   or sensory   censorship

Golden Shovel of Ignatius Valentine Aloysius' In meditation I sit still

Water Speaks

All day & night, our small fountain's
                          water rises, falls, sings, & we
listen for the life our sleepy backyard
                          brings around the trickling: insure
a public feast, this fairy water, the
                          intelligence of love's opinion & oh! the
evil that contempt wrings too with the
                          sobriety of night's hand. The world's
dying & living, giving & taking. Hunger
                          casts a grand spell just as it held
me in thrall once & I only drank, went
                          to its sources for the kill, together
hope & I discreetly watching. I do not
                          look at water now as that other thing by
the wayside, always there springing from
                          mouths of stone or pipe—it's holding
us to the future, or not or not. The accidental
                          discharge of water happens in our
dreams, impartial to bodies keeping it down.
                          Water goes where deep histories
don't want it gone, like that man on the
                          Purple Line train standing stunned in
silence as piss trailed along his jeans, like
                          the time in summer when I tore our
bathtub drainpipe with an electric plunger
                          & learned hard lessons. I see bodies
of water doing deadly things around the
                          world, its roaring mileage isn't letting
go anytime soon. I'd cancel all appointments
                          if I were you. Keep loves, keep them
embraced in the deep night, each body
                          a swift ripple. Water's rising up to speak.

Golden Shovel of David Allen Sullivan's un/delineated

Wouldn't Give

Survivor joins white-suited rescue workers on Syria's Coast near the flooded city of Derna (see photo).

Al Jazeera

water	surges	up	legs	we	keep
watch	as night	darkens	around	us	loves
were mis-	placed	& now	no one	knows what	keep-
s welling up	bodies	bruises	as if	any one of	them
a chance	survive(or)	could be	proof that	the givers	embraced
given	lives(laves)	childhoods	only	survive(al)	in
wheels	of memory	Derna	remembered	is not	the
same as	Derna	flooded	the ocean	not so	deep
bodies	washed up	we tied	each toe &	blue	night
transformed	those white	tags that	whisper	names	each
wears(weirs)	clothes	tattoos	jewelry	now just	a body
where	these	yellow boots	push down	muck	a-
wash my	sodden arms	stink of	sloshed	sewage	swift
tide surge-	deposits	another set	at our	feet thick	ripple-
s forth	frothy	(of)wave	over-	turned	water's
spilled out	rancid	dead hands	turn while	they are	rising
to help	another	pasty limbs	flesh wet	sponged	up
the ocean	& now	released	screamless	we are	to-
o late	always their	open mouths	now	only waters	speak

Golden Shoots & Ladders of Ignatius Valentine Aloysius' Water Speaks

The language of memory

The day has hit its busy high, dragged me
                    into its evidence. Spirit givers
want me to settle down now & write
                    a little, in peace, though I embraced
those same intentions when I woke up
                    but struggled apparently. My given
life did not mean much to me once, if
                    that is ever such a thing, should lives
simply go on as they are if we do little
                    for our bodies, except probe childhoods'
hungers to the fullest & witness our
                    public scrutiny as adults. See, I'm only
drifting towards the grand ceremony, not
                    snatched back to it yet, so I survive
with some faint sense of meaning, each
                    quizzing step more curious of words in
overtones going through many drafts,
                    while I wear clothes spun from wheels
of false currency. The full picture in view's
                    a compromise, the language of memory.

Golden Shovel of David Allen Sullivan's Wouldn't Give

Wholly

—for Jules, hiking together at Pinnacles

Moth-eaten leaves, filagreed above where I
lie, perforate the sky. What if I could wear
all my wrongs, if the holes in my clothes
showed all I've burned through? Airy tales I spun
to keep others at bay? Who was I hiding myself from?
When I confessed fuck-ups & addictions the wheels
turned, but each friend said they knew I was of-
f somehow—stories too good to be true. False
Evidence Appearing Real, AAers say. My currency
was a shipwreck of shoals. I claimed to know the
lay of the rocks, but I was the fool captain, too full
of myself to see through the holey picture
postcard. See these overhead leaves incised in-
to airy nothings?—what if *through* is the view?

Golden Shovel of Ignatius Valentine Aloysius' The language of memory

The Elegy Fund

If you ask me about the welfare of this stolen country, what
I know, I'll say, is all that makes me want to go insane, as if
the words we'd share about it are better said anonymously, I
dunno. What exactly do I feel right now? If all my students could
read my decades-long PTSD (my life as that!), no safety I wear
is sufficient enough to hide my shapelessness; a week from today, all
I see & want will soon be forgotten in myriad distractions, my wrongs
reminding me that it's always time for some giving, especially if the
shape of the world seems less warm & fuzzy. Indigent heart: holes
marked by failures, fought prejudices, few patches of success in my
honest days, are enough to make me talk...with silence. Old clothes
are more trendy for harboring such moods, I think. Now I showed
you how far I'll go, but not what I'd do. I'm not unfair like that; all I've
got I'm turning over to laughter & the elegy fund. Everything's burned
up in the spirit of a single day & nothing worse dare slip through.

Golden Shovel of David Allen Sullivan's Wholly

II.

Reconceive the Leaves

Attention Paid

—for Tia

Junco brushstrokes the gutter's lip & everything's
transformed if I pay attention. This burned
cloud edge, light tipped, seems ready to flare up—
so I let it be the scrawled apology I flung in
the fire, the one that enumerated all that the-
re'd been between us, all I'd squandered. Spirit-
ual was what I'd named it, but it was seeded too of-
ten with needs & greeds. When I spoke of our love, a
bird died in my chest, a fire fizzled out. Single:
the word I didn't want to own. I was headlong, day-
long, plotting my redemption in a solar flare &
nebula of new birth. I was clueless. I stopped at nothing
to convince you I was better than I was. We were worse
for wear: highway shredded tires, struck crows. How dare
I try to blame you for my shoddy acts, my caustic slip-
s? The cloud's a light trough, see what breaks through.

Golden Shovel after Ignatius Valentine Aloysius' The Elegy Fund

Self-portrait of a Virus, or a
Person Contemplating Trauma

There are dark forces still at play
                 & winning daily. I know that I
shouldn't feel sorry for myself as
                 I do. Somewhere, a place was
a paradigm of healthy existence,
                 then a chainsaw went headlong
& cut down this place, which was
                 much older than a human day,
witness to skilled hands, babies,
                 master plans. Dark forces rose, long-
ing for the heart's favor, its cold
                 aching confidence. I'm fine plotting
ways to exit the corrupted interstate,
                 mirages of hope dull beyond my
sight. Haven't I caused enough damage
                 already? Faults & redemption
go hand-in-hand, see! The open sky's
                 a mistake if it locks me here in a
desperate time. I want us to examine
                 our conduct. Mine was a solar
burst I cannot take back, though its
                 effects have hurt lives, flare(s) &
breaths collapsing, memberships
                 lapsing due to me. Time's nebula
is there, urging me inward. Maybe my
                 worth rezones paths of new
& best resistance. Maybe I'm seeing
                 my rabbit hole & hour of birth.

Golden Shovel of David Allen Sullivan's Attention Paid

For All It's Worth

> *If you've made your peace*
> *then the devils are really angels.*
>
> Radiohead, *Rabbit in Your Headlights* (video: Jonathan Glazer)

Haggard man talks to himself as he shuffles
                    through the car tunnel. He may be
houseless, & what he's cursing isn't clear,
                    but when the car veers close I'm
shivering for him—I know it's a film—
                    that this is all projection, & my seeing
myself in him is just another layer.
                    Now a group slows to tell him off & my
instinct to hit back sears. He's struck,
                    goes down squirming, a trapped rabbit
with wheels hissing his ears. He's rent
                    by a bumper, rolls, then rises, whole
& at peace. Back straightens, arms
                    unspool, he confronts the next car &
absorbs the impact as it crinkles round him.
                    This is his wolfish, stupefied hour,
this is when he sheds his scaly addictions
                    & becomes human, something of
a magician—in his deathless celluloid body's repetition
                    is my nascent re-birth.

Golden Shovel of Ignatius Valentine Aloysius'
Self-portrait of a virus, or a person contemplating trauma

Searching for Beauty

Those days when I saw my father
                talking to himself, a mind haggard
& self-absorbed by drink. I was
                searching for beauty, a too-young man
standing before closed doors at
                every turn, parents adrift, no hard talks
about school or sex, morality's road.
                In survival mode mostly, taken to
razor-thin levels. I was interested in
                things he cherished. He saw himself
in me, I was sure—our talent for art,
                soccer, music evident in us, just as
we were. But children see through screens
                of false convictions. To say he
caught my lips moving unfavorably is no
                exaggeration. How he shuffles
us like a stack of playing cards, his pet
                Rummy! The thought went through
my mind often. My search for beauty
                appealed to the warm sky, the scar,
each one, meaning to blush like a
                flower & light up the darkest tunnel.

Golden Shovel of David Allen Sullivan's For All It's Worth

Diving for Darkness

Walteria's hexactinellid sponge absorbs the clumsiness my
submersible pedal steps perform as I slow to search
along the ocean floor & determine bathymetry readings for
culling scaleless hadal snailfish whose sick slick beauty
is part of these wet dark arts.
                                    They ride thermal vents appealed
to by the court of strange contrivances, manage to
slip arms of basket stars, the gulp of toothless surinam toads, the
pinchers of shell-less squat lobsters—crevice-hid & dead warm.
Hadals ride over the wheels of anemone like an inverse sky
the E. V. Nautilus I'm in is mapping.
                                    It's as if I'm the
stretched out hand of an over-curious god or the scar
of wanting to know & name & fix in Latination. Each
chrysogorgia performs a sea aria, waving the frond of one
interconnected bottlebrush being's many branches—
                                    meaning
stretched out on these paper-thin, leafless veiny leaves to
hide brisingids, whose clawed, sea-star arms blush
red & pink while their escalators of bent spines act like
velcro & latch onto the ridges of whatever erringly nears. A
pink bubblegum coral expands its nodules & seems to flower
in response to changing light levels.
                                    I'm out of my depth, &
there's nothing here that doesn't make or hunger after a light
snack. I'm an earth-breather who'll eventually have to rise up
beyond cavernous hadal mouths. I'm the ransacker of Otherness, the
notetaker at the margins where life flourishes even in the darkest
vents.
        Recovering addict, still compelled to nose every dark tunnel.

Golden Shovel after Ignatius Valentine Aloysius' Searching for Beauty

Aperture

I wake up each morning, feeling so alive &
     glad that I'm not maimed or dead
in a world's hewn sense of loss & killings,
     those blows like all safe wheels
coming off, carrying bad news home to
     good people. Roots were mapping
spined rituals, all purpose & value kept close
     real close. If prayer-medicine's the
only course humanity takes, each selfless
     act ought to do more good & name
a new map, a kind aperture, giving clearance
     for sensitive moods to keep waving
flags of their presence. We keep learning that
     success is short-term, season's branches
spread out in fine character as long as the
     day is dry & no rain's injection. So on
we go, destined for each other's orbits and
     lit chemical sun! See all my clawed
impulses riding slow systems of joy, double-
     stepping across soft-coiled escalators
as I place one foot before the other, thinking
     of old surgeries & new ones, a life of
hard stories from the homeland & new
     life lessons advancing my discipline, coral-
sharp and just as fragile as my first moment
     of awareness. I'm held up to the light,
dead wheels mapping the name-waving branches
     on clawed escalators of coral light hunger.

Golden Sliver of David Allen Sullivan's Diving for Darkness

Set Rocking

curled cup of yellowed leaf held

    a flat of water that coughed up

a shard of sun that cut into

    my open eyes on the

earthside of seeing but the light

    kept nailing me to my

tiny minus & whispered a name's

    just a hindrance to where it's all

mushrooming up underfoot & that *I*

    turns to a frail footstool & what I have

is this have-not-ness that is a long

    fall to no one & nothing less than *&*

& *so* & *everything* until I'm belied

    by the lie of unearned blessedness as

I sink onto the hard knees of my hunger

After Ignatius Valentine Aloysius' Aperture

Flat Sun Eyes Seeing Me

In an age of disbelief, how
                did Galileo thrive, saying that flat
isn't the way to go, that we
                are round go around, adore the sun
more strictly? Judging hands
                struck down such intellects, lesser eyes
orphaned by god. I did not
                understand my schoolteacher seeing
past me, pointing towards the
                clever ones. Poverty's charge against me
had struck my prime, when all
                I wished for was to walk the grounds &
put lips to the air: What was
                my crime that I should be punished all
day long, made flat? The starving mind
                only knows its desperation, which I
followed; only knows its deference
                to sunlight, which I swear does have
its surest conditions. My lips
                went dry; cracked salt of suffering is
a mark that childhood leaves for
                the lesser-adult, who'll leave nothing
behind but an endless desire
                for respect, grand fiscal anxieties &
eyes away from prejudice.
                From where I stand, all I see are the
old burdens, flat sun eyes seeing me,
                & all I have is nothing & the sink.

Golden Sliver of David Allen Sullivan's Set Rocking

Body as Tea Cup (Broken)

Where hands flustered me they left tiny my-
      nuses—extraction points, indents on lips,
& the pressed flesh just above them that went
      in like kneaded dough, already too dry
to yeast up & become whole. So what's cracked
      open can never return to form: salt-
licks shaped by herd tongues burn. Too of-
      ten we slink & sidle away from suffering,
but what's broken open anneals new—is
      what we are. Binds of blessings hurt. We a-
tune ourselves to this new music. The mark-
      s are readable as leaves, as tats—we're that
scar they left. I try to forgive the childhood
      stripped from me to reconceive the leaves.

Golden Shovel of Ignatius Valentine Aloysius' Flat sun eyes seeing me

Home

In quiet rains of loneliness, my long
>> separation from home hits, pain points
strong-begging for attention to genuine
>> measures of the past; & quiet joy, its hand on
clearer paths, is leading me away from
>> all that disorder. I listen, as gravity's pressed
eyes roam between love's lost legends
>> & drafts of desire stored like fuel, whole
flowing worlds in retinae claiming a share.
>> I must be dead if the notes striking a cracked
life don't tremble for light & prayer; spheres
>> of dispossession branded on burnt tongues
tasting for color in salt. I must be made a
>> gentler creature away from home, that &
the extant pining is more than I can take.
>> Even seashells mark the echoes of each new
ocean tug on their backs, while immigrants &
>> machines tug at change. Emptiness is a hurt
spun down from a twining river, its truth points on
>> pressed whole cracked tongues & new hurt music.

Golden Sliver of David Allen Sullivan's The Body as Tea Cup (Broken)

Outcrossing

                             in flowers requires self-incompatibility—an emptiness
that insists on outsiderness. Recessive mutation is a hurt
inflicted on oneself, a stunting or smug stifling spun
by a kind of gamete navel-gazing, so what's put down
is self-satisfied self-satisfaction. Self-love's just a platform from
which we have to launch towards others, create a twining
that braids us in new patterned weavings, as when two river-
s blend, seeming to ride into/through each other. It's
led us to dance outside our cluster, forced us to entertain truths
that unshield us, send us into the fray—re-charging points
honed on dioecic vibrations. The habitual must be beaten on
to torque new shapes. Resource-allocation constraints press
us towards others. Catkins vibrate in the wind, seedweight cracks
them open. Flights of pollen have us speaking in tongues.
Unfolding currents churn with new-heard turns of music.

Golden Shovel of Ignatius Valentine Aloysius' Home

Pollen

41

We're sorting through all the noise
                    day after day, energy of stunting,
hard-shaped by quadrants of
                    design & sheer barbarism, so
amorphous in our mirrors in cell-
                    units completing bodies, we
stay residential. I do, it's true, more &
                    more these days, as I look to create
characters of myself in imaginary word
                    drafts that are going nowhere; each
tract more personal, more vulnerable,
                    visible like risks & a faith-dance
foreign even to myself. In all of this,
                    I'm a tragic event bee, I say this to
anyone listening, hoping to liberate an
                    unappealing guilt looming to fray
my mirrors. I'm more rural than you
                    might think, & there's us. We ourselves
rise from the arduous root-structure
                    of rebuilt driven bodies made new
in the luminary drafts of influencers'
                    vibes which we seem to watch, like
& stunting so, we create each dance
                    to fray ourselves new like pollen.

Golden Sliver of David Allen Sullivan's Outcrossing

Mirrors/Minotaurs

—after Cocteau's Blood of a Poet

Addictions replicate our self-same tropes, claustrophobically shaped
by what we've come through/where to/how soe'r—molded by
our stunted belief that danger lurks in the quadrants of
the maze we've made, that our obsolescence is by design
our own hands crafted with a click & drag, explosives tiled &
planted under bland surfaces, so to step out confidently is sheer
madness. How did we manage to manufacture such barbarism
that mangles every destiny? Look at the mirrored walls, so
smooth we see every follicle & hair on our amorphous
features replicated there, but when we reach out—in our
belief that coldness & hardness will meet us—the mirrors
melt, become liquid, & we pass wetly through in cell-units
that infinity away from this trap. There's no completing
this edifice, we exit it when we relinquish our hungering bodies.
Shaped by quadrants of design & sheer barbarism, we're so
amorphous our mirror cells unite, complete our nascent bodies.

Golden Sliver of Ignatius Valentine Aloysius' Mirrors

Conjecture

If there's one path of resistance left,
            something I can hold on to, it's the belief
that time has engineered the biography
            of the courtroom, sieges crafted with
precision, while planned backfires surge to
            acquire the winning. We're made bland
as poor fiction, tender brush & grass dispatched
            while temperatures rise. Pure madness!
Every part of my being's forced under
            construction, collapsing gradually like how
committees come apart. If there's a clear
            line to sanity, my salted sight says we
are all under investigation; though some cannot
            see it yet. The faith I took home is a reach
that's more work than is worth, & I'm
            just a fair businessman who finds out
too late like my father had, that my campaign
            of sudden awareness can melt
like a fleeting idea on the run. Everywhere
            I turn there's a crime, criminal gone from
evidence & cold as the Bering Sea. Cold as
            the stories I wrote which readers this
year await. Conjecture is belief with bland
            madness, how we reach out, melt from this exit.

Golden Sliver of David Allen Sullivan's Mirrors/Minotaurs

1. That Being the Case

Whereas sentences stick & stones are thrown; whereas
those who came before you were downtrodden, poor
as sand-extended cement; whereas your suffering's a fiction
we're not buying; whereas what was once tender
is now hardened flesh. Our kind has all had to brush
our uniforms free of your fingerings; your hand-
s on us are an affront (unless you're our dresser). The grass
that buoys up our bootheels is reluctantly dispatched
to soft-pedal the obscene stain of your graves. Whereas
our uplift occurs at precisely calibrated temperatures
that would beggar your sweat, yet you must rise
when we pass—& bow & scrape; whereas it's
necessary that you be present so we appear pure;
be it therefore resolved: our need for you is madness.

Golden Shovel after Ignatius Valentine Aloysius' Conjecture

2. Carceral Architecture

*After American Artist's Security Theater: CCTV cameras, AI, 4K monitors,
television mounts, and phone security pouches.*
Guggenheim's exhibit Going Dark: The Contemporary Figure
at the Edge of Visibility.

Seed something, stay something. While salted
inside the Guggenheim's snailing spiral in sight
of a wire-hung sleek black sphere—a tingling says
it's a many-eyed spider, tracking us—& when we
surrender our cell phones to black pouches we are
permitted inside a curtained-off room where all
our images flash on screen banks. Everyone's under
surveillance by these mechanical eyes' ocular investigation.
Our cells have been stripped, so we can only gawk, though
the question hangs: who's being monitored? by whom? Some-
one's being panopticoned—someone not us. But we cannot
not know that what sees them could just as well see
us—hear us, seize us. Each device tracks. We're under it-
s scrutiny even if our legality isn't under question—yet.

Golden Shovel after Ignatius Valentine Aloysius' Conjecture

Words I Heard Once This Season

If sentences come w/o the rifle of illness,
                        blowing pink salmon offers, these sentences
easily knock down charged pillars of doubt
                        running grizzly through my wires. I came
looking for a physician to heal my pains &
                        ate potatoes like a boat going down fast as
fame also flashes, sparking on a rippling
                        old river, age clinging to big suffering's
molecules. If sentences come countering
                        w/ absolute necessity, words I heard once
this season, ring gleaming against un-
                        glamorous vegetables in hand, so (un)kind
during the next season & thereafter. Gray
                        wolves know the condition of fire, its affront
jack-knifing the grizzly charge, too. We are
                        dynamic bodies pressing trophy buoys
at each other. The cup breaks & that's that;
                        it doesn't talk back at all like your
stretch of injuries exhibit in plain view.
                        Self-examination always makes me sweat;
I haven't been a winner of anything for a
                        little while. But victory is yours, & you
alone know its patient pair of pliers
                        rippling for dry leaves which appear
gold. Sentences came as suffering's once kind
                        affront buoys your sweat; you appear resolved.

Golden Sliver of David Allen Sullivan's That Being the Case

Bits of Blue Paint Grace One Wing

—for Chuck Atkinson

I'm drawn to the cracked & crazed
                    & wrung out, to winged victory
plowing through folds of Greek
                    himation that flare behind those ris-
ing legs that churn through seas
                    of liquidy marble—do you see yours-
elf in the headless, flapping presence?
                    Are you this heedless body &
clipped bits of prow that it commands—
                    while, with sandaled feet you
kick at bits of broken stone drapery?
                    You strive on, never alone,
though the doctors say your
                    condition cripples, what do they know
of the Greek idea that attitude's
                    manifested in what someone does? It's
your tenacious hold on this threadbare
                    life that rips apart their patient
prognosis, spits at their puffed-up
                    pontificating. Behind you that pair of
stone-soft wings are whipped by history's
                    storm like wrenched opened pliers
that grip all that's given, & against
                    the rising wind the cloth's rippling—
nothing's going as planned, but you're in it,
                    seamstress of distress, leaning for-
ward into whatever comes next, into wild storms
                    that buffet—but the hell with dry-
ness—let icy needles pierce you, you're what's
                    coming, you're what never leaves.

Golden Shovel of Ignatius Valentine Aloysius' Words I Heard Once This Season

What Quits & What Keeps Adapting

A commercial jet streaks across the sky,
    leaving contrails white cloudy & straight; I'm
still as a blank page open to new writing, my hands
    gripping the wheel while I drive, eyes up, plowing
furrows through heron blue. Like a child, launched
    by questions thin as cat's whiskers, I work through
my curiosity about jet fuel exhaust, the cold air up there,
    what quits & what keeps adapting. Funny, I'm the
most changeable thing down here, going in through
    the coming-out way in life, catching bitter clipped
signs favoring a sniffling journey, hidden mines
    along the way. Years of mail from home, once broken
dispatches wrangled like an abdominal wound, have
    given the long death its hunger. I claim this condition
so well, was once truly wealthy with helpless anger—
    & isn't this the loneliest bitten advantage of life
when civilization hands you a few chump nuggets?
    Big stakes, human! Go around again, pontificating
that socks with big toe holes are just fish on your feet
    with eyes bold like dazzling rubies. I follow history's
contrails, tumbling in the family's icy vapor tracks left
    bending, quitting as I watch; possession's a grip as
weak as an idle fishing line in a discontent stream. Best to
    keep reaching, exhibit strengths I can move (to)ward
now. I'm plowing through the clipped broken condition
    of life pontificating history's grip as ward needles.

Golden Sliver of David Allen Sullivan's Bits of Blue Paint Grace One Wing

48

Cash it All In

Handcuffs forced him to double-down
                    & peel off those dirt-soled socks
in the courtroom so he could show
                    how he'd work the shotgun with big toe
fishing for distant trigger. This sixty-
                    something had robbed a bank, shot holes
in plexiglass—video of a cartoonish
                    yellow rain slicker's recoil—the area
already cordoned off by the time the
                    teller he'd ordered out threw keys: *Just
take it!* she'd cried, running back inside,
                    then locking them all in—fish
in an aquarium. They schooled to
                    watch him get in the Prius. Turn it on.
& sit. 3 minutes. 4. Saw him fish in the
                    glove, remove the manual. *Your
car's awful quiet,* Stacy giggled, *poor soul
                    don't know to press with his feet
& just go.* But then he did. With a jerk
                    as sirens sounded. Video shows eyes
skittish as a netted shark. He drives
                    two blocks, then pulls over, bold-
ly props the door open: *To do myself in
                    for terrorizing those poor women, but like
a doofus I bungled that too. Blam! that cop
                    tackled me, sock in hand—he was dazzling-
ly quick, I give him that—but she swore
                    we'd marry if I got 'er some Burmese rubies.*

Golden Shovel of Ignatius Valentine Aloysius' What Quits & What Keeps Adapting

The Furrowed Soil Lends Its Voice

Now is the right time. Now! I'll ditch their open season on
      social media traps, their ulcerating news-fireworks. I'll peel off
the decaying covers of a writer's dead music & descend into
      a garden of words, turn rich soil into handsome seals before this
day is done. The glint of an idea so young, reveals its critical
      condition if I don't serve nourishment at its roots, let snappy rain
admit belief in a new sentence being born, then another, more as
      hope emerges in a spry week. I accept this, keep the game running
before trolls of doubt stamp their footprints across an acute
      voyage that never forgets each minute's mother, remembered in
dirt's sound of the dance which is everything! The soil's music
      owned my foiled father who suffered impatience. Drink cut him
fully from the beginning, while we stayed down with knees
      to the ground & bare hands knowing their work's capacity on
getting to the finish line—whatever that is—ea. dug-up patch with a
      lungful of scars lodged between redemption & the weakening of him.
If time's the measure of motion, then deep soil's readiness makes no
      exception second to second: *Here are your pages,* it says. *Your
turned, furrowed, nurtured, poked, fed & clipped words are doing
      something, have become something of a legion in themselves; soul
searching is a dark theater gambling for an audience.* These words rise,
      grains of sound, a rudiment of windgusts reaching like friends with
store-bought panic, their cars parked in the company's paid lot. I am
      often like them, trying to understand but watchful of gin-sirens
screaming to the tribe on weekday mornings. Garden weeds must be
      removed. But what if the weeds are inside me, perforating my eyes
locked to dad's rough cast & memory's deep trenches? Peel off this
      rain running in him, on him. Your soul with sirens eyes the door.

Golden Sliver of David Allen Sullivan's Cash it All In

Looking for Me

—Luna Maria Barivan, born-died January 4th, 2004

You painstakingly paint my blued body into a corner I never
ran to. You acerbically ache, believing everyone forgets
but you. You garland my body with flowers—each
a dying, cut-throat crime—bleeding red for a few minutes,
then blithely withering. You watch my watchful mother
wash my hair for the first & last time. I'm remembered
in slant rhymes, bullet wound moons, uncut nails—exist in
interstices, in light scuttling leaves, dry ditches. I own dirt's
spade thrusts that carve rude openings. Slices of sound
semaphore your frowning, forensic mouth. You're one of
the self-annointed grave diggers of sorrow. You're of the
earth I chew. You're nothing special. Really. The dance-
s I'm doing sashay their way past death—which is
a window, through which I see you, then everything.

Golden Shovel after Ignatius Valentine Aloysius' The Furrowed Soil Lends Its Voice

One Special Way Through

Can one truly come back from deep loss, look way
          past death & move beyond exposures that paint
the universe's grand vision for us? I know pain
            is a lungful of poor luxury, schooling near everyone
for the high price of a starved grand piano; but it's
            the instrument's sorrow which the body sings with
pitch tuned finely like honey dripping on a tongue.
            I have learned how to touch defeat, visions of red
rolling turmoil through the politics of this heart. I &
            the world would appear stronger, more watchful
of pernicious patrons itching to go hunting, since my
            desire is yet immune to such plans. I'm keen if rhymes
invite the steady examination of a stone's rippled soul
            & art. Denial can't do that, kills towns bathed in light
soft-printed against the surest circuits of truth. I hope to
            flee when pianos start falling from believed openings
in the sky. One might actually resign from loss, find a
            cause through death's long run like paper's age, one
new score sweeter than the last. Life reveals pathos, as dark
            stones inside us depart & clear passages in special way-
spells of desire, saying: *Paint everyone with red watchful*
            rhymes in light openings one special way through.

Golden Sliver of David Allen Sullivan's Looking for Me

Pourquoi me réveiller

When the tenor pries open his mouth
                every body of water in the house sinks deep-
er—aches to join stretched strings, vibrate
                in time with a man's mad list of loss-
es. Each of us shorn of love (again), every
                dredged up past that rises is a lungful of
impossibilities, of if-onlys, of could-haves.
                What'd lain dormant in us, starved
by lack of attention, rushes through his
                open mouth where strings trip like pianos,
lids opened, belly-wires plucked. Each
                orchestra member handles a ham radio tuned
to the same station. Our loves rush the
                concert hall, their perfumes suffocate like honey'
s sweet-sticky lay-away plans—we're bears,
                fur coats shiver off stings as we mine the heart
of the tree, gold-leafed by drones, honeycombed
                with seasons. We claw up honey calcite stones,
munch through mountains our bodies
                know, gnaw sorrow's wax bite—& light'
s deep loss is a lungful of starved pianos, tuned,
                like honey heart stones, to light openings.

Golden Sliver of Ignatius Valentine Aloysius' One Special Way Through

Scalpel

At every turn of my eye is a rich event, each
one a yoke or pupil's dream, electrons of us
taking market share or mallet, frosts shorn of
their will; & how the poet thinks love (again),
like trees blooming in early spring & every
seed tiptoeing around stones, roots dredged
from packed earth recording minutes, all up
for discussion, balance, the sun. This poet's past
is a close call of old odd metrics & melts that
seek advice from grassy slopes. Ambition rises
heavy as monsoon-rain's sudden cut. Work is a
credit to my heart; its fine rooms farm a lungful
of theories about topics to write about, sort of
& because art's scalpel deters impossibilities.

Golden Shovel of David Allen Sullivan's Pourquoi me réveiller

III.

Born from Shells & Tinder

My Irish Great Great Grandfather, Turned Away from Ellis Island, Entered the United States Via Canada

Sleán blade thrust severs crust. Every
root dangles like an unfinished dream.

Bog turf's hefted, barrowed home, shorn of
its place in the world. We make do with love

born out of what we're cut from. Turf blooms
& smokes in the fireplace where roots

hiss & spit wetness from compacted earth
that's been unseated. Air pockets &

the shed shells of insects sizzle & melt.
What once was living, green & grassy,

now withers into tinder. Unintended cuts
appear in the family cloth. We must farm

what we find. Burn dross. Abstract theories
lack scent. The peat stinks & scalpels possibilities.

Every dream, shorn of love, blooms roots from earth &
melts grass' sudden cuts. Farm theories scalpel possibilities.

Golden Sliver after Ignatius Valentine Aloysius' Scalpel

Heart, a Patched-Up Place

A dark beetle on the living room carpet
                cleverly plays dead, like every
prowling resentment I kept that ran from
                a cup chasing an unfinished
length. If catch & release is how to
                fend off mild home invasions, place
is my heart cooking up ways to overcome
                its dark traps & intrusions, born
before I took my first breath. Somedays,
                I fail to remember I came from
rich hardship, w/ nothing to our name
                mostly, a family broken up like shells
trampled on the shoreline, cut down
                to sand, place liquored hot & tinder-
fresh. It's what we burn that hides our
                secrets, what we catch, collect that cuts
the light falling at our feet. Another beetle
                runs, plays dead. I go after what
can be caught then let go. This place leaks,
                has wide fine holes, patches we
think have character, but no it's not that
                at all. We'll no more kill than burn
up. Every unfinished place born from
                shells & tinder, cuts what we burn, lack.

Golden Sliver of David Allen Sullivan's My Irish Great Great Grandfather, Turned
Away from Ellis Island, Entered the United States Via Canada

Lured by Smoke Smells

The black charred & coaly outback attracts Australia's fire beetle
whose pyrophilic nature pushes past aching human resentments
to descend on burnt landscapes where it feasts, lays eggs—invader
of grounds others run from. Prey gone, it flourishes—like my heart—
on what others deem a wasteland. In grift & neediness I took
what was injured & ate. I hid in ash, speckled with broken shell
bits, disappeared from sight. & when hot winds liquored
around my agile legs my thermophilic nature mined the cuts,
oblivious. I was at home in guttered gray landscapes, played
bone flutes of blackened lizard, eased hot wind through the holes
to orchestrate an elegy for softer hearts that ran or were burned.
I needed nothing but ash's gift—suffering was my heart's tinder.
A beetle's resentment invaded my heart, took broken shells,
liquored cuts, played holes, burned tinder.

Golden Sliver after Ignatius Valentine Aloysius' Heart, a Patched-Up Place

Persistence

I'm reflecting on my immigrant trauma,
       on measured dreams suspended then burnt
of imagined possibilities w/ remarkable
       delay & fashion, like those three large eggs
wasted at Sunday's breakfast once. Look,
       this really happened! My last three eggs gone,
because forgetting is body's age when it
       simply fails to understand, fails to remember a
hot skillet's task. Should eggs be held
       morally responsible then in my wasteland(s')
staggering claim? How I'd contributed
       foolishly with desire & flesh's hot neediness
clearing my escape from morality's firm
       pledge, w/ every day's play, its need, held in sight
so plainly. It became my undoing. My
       actions needed reflection & cool control when
progress whispered, seeming to appear, if
       only too slowly w/ each learning. If every hot
wedge towards survival cut bad, I always
       remembered that, acknowledging all my mined
treatments that made good with each job done.
       Everything was a struggle, everything flat gray
for so long, but maybe it's the grayness
       of everything that gives each starving bone
its true register over time. I hear the warm
       timbre of persistence come, hear its snake flutes
& faint signals of a homeland not yielded yet.
       Life is much too present, asking me to orchestrate
it. Burnt eggs gone, a wasteland's neediness in sight,
       when hot mined gray bone flutes orchestrate suffering.

Golden Sliver of David Allen Sullivan's Lured by Smoke Smells

Bipocticity

When you fled Mumbai did immigrant trauma
steal you eighteen-year-old bones? Who imagines
TV-beamed dreams come true? The staggering
syntaxes rankled, steely eyes stared, all escapes
blocked. Tongue thickened on English, moved slow
as the translating mind that doubted whether gray
matter could master it all. But your persistence
rattled bars that kept you out, as you came to understand
bars that drew you in were places where mind-bones
cracked open & liquored your immigrant sufferings.
Immigrant trauma imagines staggering escapes, slow
gray persistence & mind-borne sufferings.

Golden Sliver of Ignatius Valentine Aloysius' Persistence

Dissolve in the Flickering Neon

My friend, the immigrant's endless
             trauma is marked as two-fold: split tongue
sensing the burn-temperature of a
             hard past& heavy present, foul-thickened
by events blushing away over time. I'm
             tired. Lead feet advance daily on English
as new American ways become exposed
             from beneath. Memory's needle moved
more feverishly when opportunities
             dissolved like raw brown sugar, each slow
turn of the spoon stirring-awake my
             Kundalini, stark coiled sun, fiery as the
fever guarding this exacted body. My
             Americanness signs a bleep, translating
survival's chapters into parodies of want.
             I ask: Freedom is what?... & the mind,
a job's full-time mind? I wished for it
             but not the desk. Wrong path. I saw that
success for me was a time-release pill, clicks
             of brief jobs, paychecks that doubted
their own proof at the bank, written by
             Mad Men playing with my fire; whether
an immigrant's trustworthiness is ever in
             question, look back! Rogues shake gray
in suits in puppets' hands & the immigrant
             watches the show. What matter(s)
most is where trauma lives, for how long.
             Speak of it in whispers. Memories could
burn out, I worry. The mind's a dry match
             that first sets itself on fire, to master it
once & show how it's done. My godmother
             leaned in, her sari on the stove, lit all.

Golden Shovel of David Allen Sullivan's Bipocticity

Every Surface Visible

from Chicago's L records losses & loves: *Ray's the
straight fire. Marry me Romona. RIP Mama.* The mind's
feints & wants are graffitied on flat-roof-sealed lips, a
registry of those who've passed, & those who persist, dry
heave of what hurts or might heal. Tonight a single match
makes the rounds of Ashland street taggers's cigs that
have them fist-bunched. Sparked, they fan out, cans first
shaken, then *ssss*-snaking out letters to rival sunset's
day-glo riffs. I'm stranded on the platform—itself
a palimpsest of names & claims—witness to the on-
set of their ask: *Why R we the 1's in the line of fire?*

Golden Shovel of Ignatius Valentine Aloysius's Dissolve in the Flickering Neon

Teaching Me

My body moved unconsciously through
                the city, decades & days spent in Chicago's
unseen animus as it pulled, reaching for
                my drive & determination. If I set aside the fire
that brought me here from the homeland,
                it was because my immigrant stupor & wants
caught no distinct roots, had none here. The
                always-learning, searching, tripped my pride, those
hopeful, hard efforts. A friend employed in
                advertising once said that, sadly, educators who
teach do so because they can't find real work.
                I'm paraphrasing her, but that stung. Yet, I persist
in academia, the long road leaning first into
                design, then software, now writing. Break or make
your story, I believed, a life so layered, too
                tangled up w/ its steep learning curve, live sparks
arcing off mistakes my parents would lose no
                sleep over, back at home. I so miss them, but then
this city'd subdue & devour them if I flew
                them in, its animus pushing laser-cut letters to
go writing their unsweetened years, like mine. I
                dig the blues; Koko Taylor & Buddy Guy'd riff
too brilliantly. Chicago's fire wants those who
                persist or make sparks then letters to riff names.

Golden Sliver of David Allen Sullivan's Every Surface Visible

Anyone Can Be Anonymous

My life, brushed by ghosts, began when I left my
body & weaved my way into all these bodies—
moved by their trance of being, until we all moved
unconsciously, like dolphins riffing unconsciously
through their liquid medium, surging through
the sheer surface tensions that buoy us up, the
city an ocean of yearning & churning. The shitty
decades dropped away, those undone decades,
days searching after schools, feeling unruly, & days
spent learning how to bend/break rules, time spent
in the shunting, graffiti-splattered L cars, in
Chicago's hyphenated communities, Chicago's
unseen guests rising like stubborn ghosts, unseen
animus spray paints a derelict car, whispering: *animus*.

Double-handled Golden Shovel of Ignatius Valentine Aloysisus' Teaching Me

Moved by Their Trance of Being

A Cento

In each bone, the breath of a boy who was once my brother.

I could
        choose the path of forgetting...

In the city of the dead
there is no time
but many moments
        I'm not there anymore, am I?
                Nonsense, learn to wade through
                the heavy lack of music

When he was only a child
        in this life, my brother was wounded enough
I mean wound is another word for amenable,

for progress, for portal.

        There was
no censure then, nor was there praise.
           He
gives into it. He continued like this for many years.

days searching after schools, feeling unruly, & days
spent learning how to bend/break rules,

           Mindfully dark, why the sums, gazer?

youth's porous detour   droop-troupe
dumb fumes

Time is feral after all yet trackable

                              I know loss's idiom
                a family's gills will fail

There's a smell of diesel in the wake. I'm left in the slow
rolling
                                        in the slow
rolling...

In each bone, the breath of a boy who was once my brother.

I could
        choose the path of forgetting...

                        Never mind
            that the bruise from such a severance
            might not heal.

                        As for grief & death—we
            can scratch the sign for *door* on sheets
            of gypsum.

            We can have salt, perhaps.

Rilke wrote: *That I gently wipe away the look of suffered injustice*
            sometimes
hinders the pure motion of spirits a little.

                        In this world,
the cold, hard bread of the moon leaves

a trail for the broken to follow. They come to the water
looking for a thistle, a lily; silver shoots along its hairline.

[Source texts: Mark Wunderlich, Luisa A. Igloria, Kristi Maxwell, Christopher
Stewart, Joseph Harrington, Faisal Mohyuddin, Susan L. Leary, & David Allen
Sullivan]

Wrest from the Nest
A Cento

A fetal heartbeat
will change every-
              thing,
                  nothing.

Was there anywhere,
any
    where we could
             or should
                  flee to?

We're inside a flower,
under a pollen of stars
               vast as scattered sand.

Chicago South Side skies bleed —
not like watercolor,
             not like a wound,
                   not
like a fat, bitten plum,
             but all night,
sleepless,
     wild,
punch drunk,
            addicted to real life,
blank as the sky of a mind,
a root,
     neither ground
              nor placental—grew.

You began as someone
else's symptom.

Body of fear,
    body of laughing—
            on this gutted
    breaking
    globe,
            where night swarms
    with its dust
            of unnamed suns
& the sound of a human voice
                pleading.

    One terrible eye
            opens in the center
of your head
            to night's chill.

My stacks & stacks
            of near misses
    break your heart
            forever.

Come back from deep loss.

To tenderness I add my action,
& a hunger,
        a terrible hunger
                for the un-
imaginable.

[Source texts: Toi Derricotte, Diane di Prima, Yona Harvey, Aracelis Girmay, Dora Malech, Rachel Jamison Webster, Ignatius Valentine Aloysius, Rachel Zucker]

Leave the Nest, Roam Alone

Awakening in pieces, piecemeal, remembering each line
contains its own glimmering.

Hadara Bar-Nadav

The soul knows it's a good move to stay in your body. It has. Leave all
mutiny & disobedience behind. Here is authority, a barrage of stones

slaying doubt. But do you see? Publish your own destiny. The windows
you once looked through showed disorder in the world. A home in pieces

should have awakened you, as you dreamed of London, New York, even
Chicago. Imagined easy demonstrations of flesh. The soul became tense.

A campaign of injury followed, dispatches missing their mark. What's
going out, what's coming in? The soul begs for first aid, special measures

of a new mental order governing the heart. There is pain, sometimes it
feels as if it will give out suddenly. That's what tripped up your father first,

& struck again. His rioting life against each night's dream assassinations,
a soul appearing to roam. Yours does, too. A day a year, like each known

line on your palm shows its glimmering. Your departure from home meant
there was no going back, though some do return & some never leave again.

What do you remember? your soul asks. It's time, get things under control.

Everything I Touch is—& Isn't—You

—for Cherie

Light pools play over crisp leaves, each

    dry-minted, etched by shadow, known.

My finger frets the ridge of every line,

    airily redraws each leaf. I'm pushing on

each scimitar-shaped door as if it were your

    heart, as if a key was snugged in my palm,

as if pressed on nature would reveal secret shows,

    as if my attunement with leaf fall were its

fulfillment—but I'm stuck on this side, glimmering.

Golden Shovel of Ignatius Valentine Aloysius' Leave the Nest, Roam Alone

November 6th, 2024

Paul Guest

Not again, this mourning! I'm frozen with death.
Ribbons of silence tighten themselves around me.
Even the birds have gone quiet, & no one's driving
outside yet. It's like that. Sorrow & surprise come
like a trench backfiller, quickly covering up all the
hope I'd stored in there, my festival-heart, all year long.
Now I know, the night-sweats were saying my body's
weeping, my soul's weeping, my essence is weeping.
Sweetness & light quickly disinherited by darkness'
indecency. A hate-wave touched my doorstep, knocked
& wouldn't go away. Must I leave or clash, allow my-
self the perishing? I'm frozen with death. Ribbons of
goodness wrap themselves around me, reminding me
to do my work, make art, survive. It seems that all I do
is survive. I wanted joy again, wanted the leisure of a
good smile, happy teeth. Celebration! But there's little
reconciliation. What's more American than a school
ceremony full of joy, & books circulating between
libraries that won't die of natural causes? What of the
immigrant's dream? Is that not a thing anymore?
History cannot be defeated or altered. Imitated, yes.
There's a new rural class on this indigenous land; my
language cannot reach them or make peace with them.
& together we go on writing our own new histories.

November 7th, 2024

Together we go on writing our own new histories.

Ignatius Valentine Aloysius

we
marble
asured
driving
come
the curve
long
body's
weeping
darkness'
knocked
my
off
me-
do
a-
little
school
between
them
anymore
yes
my
them
histories

chisel
in
out
feathered
round
of shoulder
fall into
a graced state
while not
sinewed
off kilter
lord
hardship
nos
you mock
bout
blows
a hazard
two or three
statu-es-
leads sense-
this is
unbeginning
is us
begins with

a dent
-ured
&
wedges
contours of
a cut of
the dark
a way of
weeping
in shadows
by blows
what rude
reckless
sus brazos
me or pity
to become
tapped out
they can
jobs
que-
less
the end
has begun
unrusted
atrocities

in death
me-
calipered
deeper
flesh
meat
heart
passing
oneself
suggestion
of a hammer
form birthed
like Venus
winged victory
what we're
Othering
immigrants
ill afford
us or
masquerade
parades
then
what we call
recast hell
where hope hangs

Golden Shoots & Ladders of Ignatius Valentine Aloysius' November 6th, 2024

Sitting for Insight & the Stars

When I move I must be a monster to
the black ant near my feet, a demon
to the spider sinewed where a porch wall
turns against the light, my gestures swift
& alarming to them as the red-tailed
hawk is to me in daylight.
                              Hawk comes
sweeping into the backyard pine tree
while I sit quietly in a chair, eyes fixed
on school work. Its claws rude with death
& fresh meat. Our eyes meet, lock. This
bird of prey pumps vigilance in me, &
my heart blows a new unbeginning. This
sighting's a call: *Look deeper, remain sharp.*
Every day & second recasts victory for
one creature, hell for another.
                              What do I see
about life's journey? What am I not seeing
as clearly? *Look deeper, remain sharp.* I dare
not move, dare not pity myself till it leaves,
satisfied with fates unrusted, jobs done &
new ones begun.
                              A writer needs nothing but
a chair, both knees brought together to form a
laptop desk. Or a real desk, if sitting upright
is a better way to hammer out the dents
calipered in the spine's weeping, shunning
hardship cut from boulders.
                              Hazard away
nothing, except the mind's own masquerades.
Sitting contours a graced state, appears so,

but it's slowly chiseling a lane that hazards
dark measured wedges birthing an off-
kilter ride. The body weeps with its own
darkness, light tapped-out little by little,
learning of its red-feathered senses, though
it can ill-afford staying in the shadows for
much too long.
         Between that & a passing
of parades, hope comes knocking, *lordy-
lord!* blowing across my shoulders to say,
"Look up at the stars once in a while. They
come & go like your words on the page."
I long for such suggestions, welcome what
I'm about to become & say "Yes!"
               I'm here,
sitting to quiet my mind, fall into statuesque
states driving away from an end, from chaos
that comes curving around the corner. I've
caused so much chaos in the past, & for that
I'm terribly sorry. I'll take the *othering*.

With words from David Allen Sullivan's November 7th, 2024

There's a Darkness in Me that Helps Me See the Light

I push back dark, but what I turn from I've
become. My unswallowed darkness caused

the ink that fills night's pens to run so
thick with sorrow's gooey stench that much

of what leaches out is word gibberish chaos,
as if wind-whipped crows flipped in

mid-flight, careened around a tree trunk in the
flightpath & caromed back into the past.

We're all one. We're what we've come for—&
when they come for us, everyone's done for.

An electric blanket of crows blots the sky like that,
they recall haunted carrier pigeons that I'm

discovering online. I hope that knowing our terribly
taut past can make our future less sorry.

Golden shovel of Ignatius Valentine Aloysius' Sitting for Insight & the Stars

A Degree of Sensitiveness

An electric blanket of crows blots the sky...David Allen Sullivan's
There's a Darkness in Me that Helps Me See the Light

The emails come like a barrage
on a cloudy & cold Monday morning,
lightning knives strafing my pencil-thin awareness
making asks for new meetings, contributions,
recommendation letters, application reviews,
many stating announcements & event reminders.
So over the top, I intuit. I avoid filtering.

Pursuit & matter raise the bar once again,
because I've been sought-out, found
& because I chose to get involved.
I'm a fraught mark of our species, one breath away
from inked heaviness, one eye engraved
with the poorest hindsight.

The modern-day lulu is a multitasker,
so I should know...so
get on with it, I tell myself. *Quit a panic!*

My heart begs for no facsimile
of an invented apocalypse,
but sharp blades of doubt soon come
like a blanket of crows obscuring the skies.
Again, I go running in the grain
as blue ink will do
on the landscape of a clear page.

I'm searching for some true character in myself,
one that can re-occupy new indelicate changes jolting me.

There's a joke hidden here
about my own shade, my incessant play
& blindness regarding change—
What I learn from it or don't.

Even so, it's rhapsody that I desire,
& rhapsody's always in flux, though
I feel it rising when I carve out time for poetry
first thing each morning.
That's when I begin unlinking my reach
with etched mysteries of deep dreamy nights,
inert hours when I'm not in this world.

Who's pulling the sheets at my feet,
passing deep chills through my unconscious body?

In time, I'm ready to
start answering emails in no particular order.
I give them light, give them satisfaction that's never
just black & white, sometimes
facing some exposition, incoming or outgoing.

Where do influence & candor fall? I wonder.
How am I perceived by the one reading my answers?
I'll never know
as I'll never know if a day's work is ever fully done.
Expressions just go quiet, trail off,

& each day my hairlines move,
quietly rendered like my faith in a kind &
less ensnaring world.
If my soul shows its spiritual nascency,
that's only natural.
My eyes beg for more light,
& I'm not quite done chasing the electrified muse.

Night Thaw

—for Jeanne & Annie

Powderhorn park's pond's a calm, icy blue
under mist last night's rain left—but black ink's
spill slides nightfears from my dark time to land
them here, & here—islands of frazil-scape
that make contorted countries bumping on
shore's edge—ice sheets fractured—as if a page
had been scarred by dream journaling. This is
what my mind mauls the world with—not
what's there, but something near—stillness not quite
still—quiet unsettlings. Mallards come undone,
weaving V's with unseen feet, dunk-chasing
after hard greens. Heads stutter, shake off the
cold melt. This morning's electrifying—
terrors re-strung by the many-mouthed muse.

After Ignatius Valentine Aloysius' A Degree of Sensitiveness

Carnival

We are given tongues as surely as we
                      have the sun & all planets, nightfears
spinning yarns about our inner spaces,
                      moving so much faster than any land
holding bodies meant to do & die. I
                      am a carnival, sent far out on shores
seemingly better than the one I left
                      breaching through. My journaling
kept me grounded, took the heat, as
                      life knocked me around, & my mind
took shelter in the idea of food—art
                      or need?—stopped on my tongue, not
a day turning w/o this adornment. Call
                      me backward, because in my stillness
my brain rides a thrill when I lick the
                      back of a spoon, like love's weaving
in & out through days of certainty or
                      nothingness. My mouth's going after
intuition & reason, using words as con-
                      traband color. If I'm caught, it's how the
nightfears land on shores journaling my
                      mind, not stillness weaving after the cold.

Golden Sliver of David Allen Sullivan's Night Thaw

Select

—for Pippin

*A muscle responsible for raising the inner eyebrow and exposing the whites
is uniformly present in dogs but not in wolves. It produces a sad expression
that often triggers a nurturing response.*
       Evolution of Facial Anatomy in Dogs
      Kaminski, Waller, Diogo, & Burrows

Wolves are our domesticated dogs mi-
nus whited eyes, while their wilder mouths
house the same teeth. What was going
to soften them? make them take after—
look after—our corralled cows? Intuition
chose communicative, plated irises & reason-
able kindnesses that they projected. Using
selective breeding, we multiplied words
for each kind that was kind, & as-
sured attentiveness was the contraband
that snuck in with the variegated colors
of softening, strokable coats. It's as if
we loved them like our hurt children. I'm
child-like too. What've my sad eyes caught?

Golden Shovel after Ignatius Valentine Aloysius' Carnival

Forty-five Years from Now?

> *Between us, a tissue of smoke,*
> *a bundle of belongings, luggage*
> *that will seem to float beside us...*
> *the currency we will change*
> *and change again.*
>
> Carolyn Forché

It's the kind of question I may have asked back then to soften
the blow of an unlikely future, asked it forty-five years ago as our
letters moved between us like tissues of smoke. My stark irises
put to work, & shock shell sentience practicing thrift, pain-using
processes cold-new to me. I couldn't tell you how change & words
distressed my need, my conclusions. I was never made ready for
this world—yet here I am with an old box of letters, attentiveness
like the smell of a new language where I'm floating for help that
comes, drawing out emotions & shaking up things. Age has snuck in
done did its dirty work, because reading about you torches time as we
soften our irises using words for attentiveness that snuck in as we hurt.

Golden Sliver of David Allen Sullivan's Select

Firing Back

—for P.G.

Stink pricks me, draws me to the window where a gluey smell
assaults. Two men, the next building over, smooth tar of a new
flat roof that'll seal in the old. They've smeared an olfactory language
that bypasses censors: I'm back in a high school locker room where
a wet paper towel laced with rancid pepper is rubbed in my eyes. I'm
flailing blind for the ones who did it. Half-naked ghosts are floating
just out of reach, sweat-rank, chanting: *Davy the Baby!* I call for help
but no one's fool enough to free this scapegoat. On my locker's a drawing
of a limp balloon of a penis, & my jockstrap's been taped out-
side with two marbles & a pencil's blunt nub inside. Emotions
are for losers—I can't afford them. I blind my way to the sink &
smack my face with water until the sting lessens. I'm shaking—
shaken. Heat from the tar roof rises, distorts my view of things:
a glove, tarred to a broom as a joke, one stiff finger pointing up.

Golden Shovel of Ignatius Valentine Aloysius' Forty Five Years from Now?

Laddering

I've seen it in birds too,
                true hard labor like poetry
                                & art pull from the seal
of an artist's heart.
                Creation's spit breeds bread
                                breathes bright in the room
like nobody's business,
                & what comes out is a
                                holy creature I'm no-where
near close to explaining
                fully, but feelings are
                                generally good. Sun, I'm blind
to the spirits in the room,
                they own me. I own this
                                fervent house, & go floating
in some unexplained con-
                dition, as birds dropping
                                down from skies, chanting
absurdly at the bird bath.
                I'm watching it now from
                                the rear window, here but
not here. It's the thing of
                the thing, you know what
                                I mean? Life's causes free
the mundane, & I'm
                laddering into my imagination,
                                say "I want!" So see my
seal, the room where
                I'm blind floating chanting,
                                but free my emotions.

Golden Sliver of David Allen Sullivan's Firing Back

The One They Nicknamed Chuchu

—for Amy Zahn, Cornell Veterinary Program

As she squealed open the metal door a dozen frozen creations
leered from the shelves: pet cadavers—half a bulldog whose spit
wedded opposing teeth like floss, & all manner of dog breeds
whose deaths newbie vets were in the process of dissecting, like
the dogs had asked for this. Caught mid-snarl, they were nobodies
anymore, shorn of names & fur. But it wasn't all business.
Amy palmed a Frankensteined pup they'd cobbled together &
marrionetted its tendons to make it trot. I laughed at what
they'd wrought. It was just meat after all. When it comes
down to it we're all mechanical—the way PT's dish it out
there's not much more to us. But there is. Amy smiles. She is
in Australia now, but I see her there. The made-up pup is a
conglomeration of discards astride her hand, & laughter's holy.
We're string-pull jobs obeying love's tug—that undying creature.

Golden Shovel of Ignatius Valentine Aloysius' Laddering

Keeping it Simple

> *I laughed at what they'd wrought.*
> *It was just meat after all.*
>> David Allen Sullivan

with a meal of hot rice, dal &
savory *achaar* is a comforting act.
This basic food's an old Asian revolution
of simple stimuli,
expressing little anxiety about
synchronicities waiting for me
around the corner, kindling
my body's unbiased triggers.

It's food I go to when I'm stressed.
Keeping it simple is simply
a good test for
                              stress.
My mother knew only *that,*
knew the harms of our indigence
& followed her hand to our mouths.
She'd make the best of
complex situations, shut out the
moral fates of this world.

We've really
complicated everything, haven't we?
Ignored the sentience of animals.
Removed cognition from
our neurotransmitters.
Exhaled war
into valences of hope &
decent prayer.
Made food a desperate pleasure.

Every heart begs for
another minute of salvation,
only I don't always know when
help comes for mine,
until after that's all done and gone.
My heart,
it wants to hum with joy, laugh
even at what they'd wrought
across the spines of their blades;
it is a meat after all.
Though my heart won't
eat itself anytime soon, because
it wagers no false history,
knows the pain of
being exploited, feeding
on dry, hot air.

Hunger needs more empathy
from the world.

Have you ever seen
or heard of a vegetarian lion?
Some animals must conspire
against the other, feed
on the pain of the cortex.
Investigate an insect with god's tongue.

Every act of feeding is a slaughter.
Even the asparagus aches
for its cut-off tip, the
broccoli goes pessimistic on
the cooked browned quiche.
Cut mushrooms moan happily—
The soft lentil too
loves a squeeze before dying.

Waiting

        in quiet spots—behind stairs, inside walls,
lodged in the black sheen lightning etched into a tree—
poems hum to themselves; in raucous arguments—
hurled between adjoining apartments; thrown up
from bus wheels, keening overhead in brutal beaks—
poems clamor in between times—before you pull
the parking brake, as the egg wobble spins
slower, while the words that seared (which you
flung back in kind) sink into your heaving
chests; the poems emit their calls—throbbing
like fireflies winking a river above a river. Don't wait
for them to come, go looking for them in the cracks
of your life, like seasonal mushrooms they push up-
wards whispering: *Spoor spreader, help us propagate.*

*

A poem that would become something, now lies
waiting like a model animal, looking up at me from
its place in the epidermic layers of my curiosity, & I
keep still staring back at it. Skin & muscle sighing for
a chain reaction of sorts, suction violating all my doubt
& taking me back to where I'd first started as a writer
zeroes ago. Isn't that the case for us rabbit types? A hint
emits a call & I go digging, a pill of prose or wordcraft
taken twice daily is brought up in an internal argument.
Well, that's one way to grass a point. There's no design to
wanting freedom in ea. verse, just the infrared intensity
of witnesses is all. Partly because, as Mary Oliver says,
we are so close to the beginnings of it. There's a poem in
every raw spot if one goes looking through whispers for it.

*

Wild horse snorts to announce its presence.
Flank waves ripple as I snag the mane
fist it tight & hoist myself astride its back.
Legs hug the muscled girth, as I press
my face into horseness. It rears, gallops off,
& I bend low, duck live oak branches as it
vaults a stream & spine ridges up into me.
I'm no centaur, we're not one creature,
mastering this isn't possible. I hold on
for dear life, wait for it to tire. Dismount
when it drops its head to muzzle & tear
the grass. Slap my hand against the vast
hillock of its neck. Dirt clouds up around
my pale, already vanishing, handprint.

*

Wild horses, poet friend! That's quite a leap (pun
intended), & perhaps *poems clamor in between times*
& you're asking me to also ride the spine of chance of
high risk levels marking poetry's pegasus leaping
from Medusa's blood. Nothing is simple or easily
understood, but everything I touch is tied, fed into cartilage
& bone & memory's annulus. What do animals remember
of their pasts that we yet don't understand? Some stay
wild, some so kind, others are quite immune to calamity.
Freeda Barker-Biter lives next door, prowling the yard
the fences on all sides, a specimen of unmuted savagery,
heated breath for what hurt her once. Now the kind hand
of an owner, who insists this mixed breed will change.
If my poetry could fall from my lips & calm her down.

*

There was a woman I briefly hitch-hiked with,
from Dover up to Wales, both in our twenties,
traveling light, we each carried a single book,
but she'd rip free read pages to lighten her load.
She relished the sudden sundering, leave the fragments
tacked to train station cork boards, in restroom stalls,
folded into origami cranes, or launched from towers
as paper planes. Sayonara pasts. So long drift verbiage.
Bye trails she loved leaving. No looking back, no loitering,
every plot turn of an ending jacked free & set sail.
Once we read a book sitting side-by-side on a train,
& near the end she tore away the first chapter
& let two deaths and a miscarriage go flapping
over the darkening heath. If I could let go that easily!

*

Once almost a decade ago, I became fixated
on syllables & attempted to write a novel by
marking accents & stresses above each word, soon
aware of patterns forming on the page, holding
me in gradually. Yet, such wonder, warm naiveté!
My patience inflamed & I got excited by the
whole experience, normalized my effort as a
cool experiment affecting my daily moods my
structure. You can see how this would disrupt the
plot at work, characters slipping as discs on a spine,
stressing the narrative's tissues. I had it all in my
head, sure of this growing animal, but the more I
fed it, the more it calcified, slowed me down. Even so
a perfect pain, comfort in words aimed at the heart.

                              *

        —for Kit Birskovich

Each day neighbors pause mid-conversation
to take in the stumbling arpeggios,
half-speed cadenzas, muddied Mozartian
melodies spilling from her grand piano.
How it transmorgraphies our hearts to know
these children are making their way across
wire fences of music staves to unplowed
fields of possibility—biting lower lips.
The seasons petal down & pass, & still
they go at it, the music springs from cells,
heads turn, ears are tickled. We lighten, lift,
walk above the walk with our younger selves,
remember when we believed songs in us
could be bodied forth, carry us like stars.

                              *

If I keep my head down, I'm not being sullen, though that's
not out of the realm of possibility, given the world's
dark asynchronous burden of tensions. I'm looking down,
is what it is, thoughts moving along some unnamed point
on the floor before me as I go about my day. What's running
through my mind is the mess of immigration. *Secret, my country
is ill*, poet Robert Haas wrote. Now xenophobia's neatly trans-
planted into the once-welcoming soul of this place. I may
never have time to run. I too am their profile of dusty lies &
remain inclined not to speak up out of caution. Everywhere,
gusts of wind raise the question of democracy & things have
really gotten out of hand. We're waiting for something to
happen, checks & balances. I live. Across the Internet, across
social media, words proliferate while scaffolding eyes raid.

*

    —for Taylor Gorman

Words thrown over your shoulder
like salt. Words lifted up for the wind
to steal. Dip your finger in the river
to write what no one will ever read.
Comb your hands through wet grass
to tell the earth your needs—or of love's
absence. Scratch desire into love's flesh.
Spell your wishes on the mouth's cave
with your tongue. Don't sign a name
to the poems you stuff in neighbor's
mailboxes. Be anonymous. Be less than
one. Be next to none, so death tastes fresh
as bread pulled from an oven, still
leavening as it burns your tongue.

*

And I ride ride I ride on to the end—
Gwendolyn Brooks

I'm the very same in you you & you, rapid flow in every
area of flesh conceived into the neonatal, little thing
grown up now & needing me preciously for its bright life. I
move too in the inchworm, soft pendant—it seeks the touch
of blue flagstone, dangles from a high branch. Trust is
all it knows, has in a hostile world. That's its freedom &
I, its gift of love. I'm the same in you you & you. Who isn't
dead yet who still cancels me? 'Sanguis' in Latin, can you
look it up & save it? I'm just another word as words go, then
why staunch me at the injury site? It's an act of love. There's
every gene of it in my expression. Shower love, share joy,
the optimal dosage passed through digested despair, dyed in
all your confused, crossed signals. I'll warm your heart's cold.
Everything I touch is & isn't you, then there's joy in cold waiting.

David Allen Sullivan's books include *Strong-Armed Angels, Every Seed of the Pomegranate, Black Ice,* & a book of co-translation with Abbas Kadhim from the Arabic of Iraqi Adnan Al-Sayegh, *Bombs Have Not Breakfasted Yet.* He won the Mary Ballard Chapbook poetry prize for *Take Wing. Black Butterflies Over Baghdad* was selected for the Hilary Tham Capital Collection by Tim Seibles, & published by Word Works Books. *Salt Pruning* was the first collaboration with Ignatius Valentine Aloysius. *Seed Shell Ash*—a book of poems about his Fulbright year teaching in Xi'an, China— is forthcoming from Salmon Press, and an anthology he co-edited with his art historian mother: *Magpie on the Gallows: An Anthology of Poems on Bosch and Bruegel's Art*, from Carbonation Press.

https://dasulliv1.wixsite.com/website-1.

Photo: Taylor Gorman

Ignatius Valentine Aloysius is a naturalized U.S. citizen, born in India and raised in Mumbai by a Tamilian father and Anglo-Indian mother. He earned his MFA in Creative Writing from Northwestern University, where he teaches. He is the author of the literary novel *Fishhead. Republic of Want* (Tortoise Books) and the collaborative poetry collection, *Salt Pruning* (Hummingbird Poetry Press), co-written with David Allen Sullivan. His third poetry collection *Bone Dust Mother* is forthcoming on Glass Lyre Press in Summer 2026. Ignatius is the current host and curator of the reading series Sunday Salon Chicago. He is the creator of Hapticwound, a one-person indie rock songwriting project, and Fab Hippo Records LLC. Ignatius is Co-Editor of *The Overturning Anthology* (Erratics Press) and serves as Co-Chair of the Curatorial Council at Ragdale Foundation, where he is also a Board of Trustees member. He lives in Evanston, Illinois.

https://linktr.ee/ignatius.valentine.aloysius | hapticwound.com